A Black Eye Isn't the End of the World

07   08   09   KFO   10   9   8   7   6   5   4   3

ISBN-13: 978-0-7407-5494-4

ISBN-10: 0-7407-5494-7

Library of Congress Control Number: 2005923697

Photography Credits

Pages i, 1, 2, 4, 6, 8, 10, 12, 16, 18, 20, 22, 24, 26, 28, 30, 32, 34, 38, 40, 42, 44, 46, 48, 50, 52, 54, 56, 58, 62:
National Zoological Park
© Smithsonian Institution
Photos by Jessie Cohen

Pages 14, 36, 60:
© Photodisc / Getty Images

Special thanks to Judy Kirkland

A Black Eye Isn't the End of the World
The Panda Principles
Simple Thoughts for a Better Life

Ray G. Strobel

**Andrews McMeel
Publishing, LLC**

Kansas City

At the Halfway—Reevaluate

Maybe you shouldn't always finish what you start.

Halfway up your next tree, pause long enough to ask yourself if it makes sense to go on. After all, the higher you get, the more you see.

And you might already have arrived exactly where you need to be right now. Ahhh . . .

Find Your Own Bamboo

Don't waste even a minute trying to pretend you love something just because others do.

Unless you decide for yourself, you'll always be hungry—starving for satisfaction and approval.

Trust your own gut, not someone else's eyes.

When You Cuddle, Cuddle with Conviction

Never cuddle with less than full effort. You'll regret it later when you remember the moment.

And remembering is often the best part of cuddling.

So share dreams. Tell secrets. Or even be silent. But do so with your paws wrapped around each other—with conviction.

When Life Knocks You Down, Nap

Be still.

Lie right where you are—hurt, stunned, bruised—and nap. Don't fight back or even try to get up. At least not right away. Let go of everything except your dreams.

Perhaps there's a lesson or two to be learned from life's disappointments, and you'll discover that a little quiet time can leave you magically refreshed . . . and better prepared to charge ahead again, with renewed resolve.

Life Is Not All Black and White

Right/wrong. Good/bad.
Yes/no. Black/white.

But not always.

Frankly, life, like a panda,
is a little fuzzy, too.

And that's good because
sometimes the blurrier the
edges get between different
choices or points of view,
the clearer we see the value
of both.

Whisper the Words

Take a break during
playtime—stop the action—
and *whisper* the words.

Don't compete with the
sounds of life. Yours are the
sounds of love.

Unusual Problems Require Unusual Solutions

When your life turns upside down, you might be scared because what worked before won't help. Don't be.

Just don't look back. You'll untangle yourself when you realize new solutions aren't that difficult. They're just new.

That kind of thinking makes it easier. You'll see.

Don't Be Afraid to Let Others See You

What's the value in others appreciating you if it isn't the real you they're seeing?

So, go ahead, put your apprehensions aside—open up to others.

Yes, it may take a little courage to let them see the real you, not just some facade. But you may just discover you're better than you think you are.

Tickle, Don't Scratch

Solo tickling is merely scratching. You'll never make it work without another participant.

It's one of life's little mysteries, or perhaps just someone's way of telling us we need others to be part of our life to make it more enjoyable.

Look at Life Sideways

Sometimes, situations aren't always as they seem.

Tilt your perspective even a little, and you may find your whole life changes.

Viewing the world from a different angle can lead to some interesting discoveries.

Even truth.

Frolic While You're Still Frolicable

Today just might be the last day you can run or jump or race around. Or frolic.

In an uncertain world, one never knows when that day might come.

So frolic hard and often. After all, you never want to find yourself waking up with frolic regret.

Long for Less

Longing hurts a bit . . . burns a bit inside. But that's okay. That's what makes it longing—not simply wanting.

So save your longing for what really matters: love, contentment, wisdom, happiness.

Want whatever you wish. *Long* for what counts.

Touch Base More Often

Life can be wonderful—then
turn on you in an instant.

The ups and downs, ins and outs,
can wear us out and drive us crazy.
Or drive us home more often.

Family is eternally there for us.
Even as it fades in one direction, it
blossoms in the other and remains
our rock—our anchor—in all times,
good and bad.

Share More Than Small Stuff

Sharing that which you have in abundance is not sharing fully—no more than a garage sale for your soul. And often as rewarding.

Share your treasures, not your spoils: your pillow, your deepest thoughts, your fears, your saddest moments, your sweetest dreams.

It's okay to take it slow—to be timid at first. It's always more difficult to share what's dear.

Sad Goes Away—Just Don't Rush It

You can't hurry sadness away any more than you can hurry away a dreary November day. When it wants to go away, it will.

Sadness won't last forever, any more than winter does. So go ahead: Let tears fall, hug your arms around a heavy heart. And wait it out.

You'll find it's easier enduring sad when you know it's just a matter of time.

Rebalance

We worry too much about rebalancing our portfolios yet fail to remember that lives get out of balance, too.

Take stock, and you may discover you are neglecting some of your most valuable assets. Pay more attention to them before they become your loss.

After all, a little of everything brings the growth you're looking for.

Circle Once—Then Climb

Some people spend their entire lives at the base of a tree.

Others start the climb.

There's a difference between assessing the challenge ahead and being frightened of the journey.

One circle of the tree is generally enough. More than that can lead to dizziness. And that's no way to get to the top.

Tackle the Trees

The world is full of easy challenges: shrubs in the forest of life. Pass them by and set out to tackle trees.

Master one small tree and forever laugh at the shrubs.

Look Under the Fur

Perhaps if, like pandas, we all looked alike, we would be less tempted to spend time analyzing the outsides of others.

We would just focus on the more important parts "under the fur," where all the good stuff hides.

For, behind even the harshest label and under the coarsest fur, isn't there a little magic in everyone?

It's Okay to Be Proud of Getting to the Top

You kept going and achieved what you set out to do. It took strength, discipline, courage, and faith (most of which you didn't even know you had).

You did it! You deserve to be proud.

So roar loud and long (when others aren't around to hear you).

Be Prepared to "Be There"

The time will come—deep down you'll sense it. You will say the words "I'll be there for you," and you will want them to be true.

Will you be strong enough? Strong for yourself as well as for others?

Be confident that as time goes by and your love grows, so will your strength to be there. Just like you promised.

A Black Eye Isn't the End of the World

Black eye? Don't be sad. Or ashamed. Everyone gets them at one time or another.

Focus not on the present stain but on the past. A black eye is only serious if you don't understand what caused it.

Learn from yours—grow—and it will soon fade, both in your eyes and in the eyes of others.

Find a Friend Who Likes the Same Things You Do

Opposites attract? Sure, but even opposites need to share a passionate interest or two. It creates a special bond that goes beyond words.

Talk is wonderful, but sometimes it can just plain wind you up and wear you out. It's times like that when we all need that special friend we can turn to—without speaking—and give, and receive, just a look that says, "Yeah, me too!"

Face Life Straight On

It's easy to turn corners in life to avoid what lies ahead.

Sometimes you still get where you want to go—it simply takes longer.

But the bigger worry is you'll get lost, and never get there at all.

An Extra Inch Is Innocent Enough

Growing is what life is all about. Outside and inside.

An extra inch or even two outside is innocent enough, especially since savoring every season of life keeps our hearts and minds growing, too.

But it's too easy to devote undue attention to the outside when it's the inside that may require more attention. Your outside is—well—just your outside.

Don't Scratch for the Re-scratch

The result is rarely this immediate, but nevertheless it is true: Scratching the backs of others often brings reciprocity.

But planning ahead to be scratched back is no way to enjoy the pure joy of helping someone else.

Scratch for the moment and not for some distant reward. Then if and when the re-scratch comes, you'll enjoy it all the more.

When Panic Threatens, Go for a Stroll

This is not the time to hit the ground running. That's what your mind is doing, and it's time to slow the pace.

How slow is slow enough? When the world around you is no longer a blur, and you can see it as clearly as the nose on your face.

Amazingly, other things will become clearer as well. And you'll discover that your speed will directly relate to the smile that will magically appear on your face.

Don't Hog the Log

Yes, you have earned your place on the log. And it's wonderful—unless you get greedy and try to keep it all for yourself.

Far better to lend a paw now so that others can return the favor, should you ever stumble.

Ponder—Profusely

How does fur know where to be black and where to be white? Why do pandas have no eyebrows?

Sometimes there are answers but more often, just mysteries to ponder.

You'll find it's the best workout for a flabby mind. Why strive for washboard abs when you could have a washboard mind?

Ponder that for a while!

Make Time to Dream

Unless you make time, you'll never find it.

Create a dream spot . . . and go there religiously. Close your eyes. Don't think—dream, and you'll discover the magic of ordinary days.